The Big Picture

English for a Globally Connected World

Myeong-Hee Seong / Daniel Cuffey / Erika Choe / Chase Karcher

지식인

Authors

Myeong-Hee Seong
Ph.D. in English Education, Korea Univ.
Professor, Eulji University

Daniel Cuffey
M.Ed. Education, University of Illinois
Professor, Eulji University

Erika Choe
M.Ed. International Education, Framingham State University
Professor, Eulji University

Chase Karcher
M.A. Cultural Studies, KyungHee University
Professor, Eulji University

The Big Picture

English for a Globally Connected World

2019년 12월 30일 초판 1쇄 발행
2024년 3월 1일 초판 5쇄 발행

지은이 | Myeong-Hee Seong · Daniel Cuffey
Erika Choe · Chase Karcher
펴낸이 | 김종욱 · 명사동
펴낸곳 | 지식인
등 록 | 제301-2013-134호
주 소 | 서울시 도봉구 도봉로 180길 20 투웨니퍼스트 102동 602호
전 화 | 02)2266-8606
팩 스 | 02)2266-8607
E-mail | jisikin2013@naver.com
홈페이지 | www.jisikinbook.co.kr

ISBN 979-11-88105-51-9 (93740)

값 12,000원

The Big Picture

English for a Globally Connected World

The Big Picture

English for a Globally Connected World

Table of Contents

UNIT 01

Different Strokes for Different Folks

Warm-up *Daily Routine (Weekdays vs. Weekends)*

Write 3 things you usually do on weekdays.

Ex. Wake up at 7:00 a.m.

1. ______________________
2. ______________________
3. ______________________

Now combine these three things into a complete sentence:

Ex. On weekdays, I usually wake up at 7:00 a.m., eat a small breakfast, and go to class.

____

____

Write 3 things you usually do on weekends.

Ex. Meet friends in Seoul.

1. ______________________
2. ______________________
3. ______________________

Now combine these three things into a complete sentence:

Ex. On weekends, I usually wake up at 10:00 a.m., drink coffee, and meet my friends.

____

____

Vocabulary Focus

A. Definition Matching. ***Write the letter next to the correct word.***

_______	1. humdrum (adj.)		A. normal; ordinary
_______	2. obsession (n.)		B. planned to serve a particular purpose
_______	3. run-of-the-mill (adj.)		C. occurring in turn repeatedly
_______	4. obscure (adj.)		D. lacking excitement; dull; boring
_______	5. strategic (adj.)		E. physical strength
_______	6. brawn (n.)		F. fixation; something you always think about
_______	7. alternating (v.)		G. having similar tastes or opinions
_______	8. like-minded (adj.)		H. not well known; not easily understood

B. Fill in the Blanks. ***Write the correct vocabulary word from above.***

1. A vacation would give me a needed break from my ___________ job.
2. Stretch your arm, ___________ between your left and right.
3. What makes him so different from the other ___________ players is his hard work and passion.
4. The army withdrew their forces for ___________ reasons.
5. My current ___________ is chess. I want to play it all the time.
6. One benefit of university is meeting ___________ individuals.
7. I need someone with lots of ___________ to move my refrigerator.
8. I have doubts about his story. It is quite ___________.

Different Strokes for Different Folks

What makes you tick? What sparks your interest? If you're like most people, you have interests outside of your humdrum academic life. You may find yourself daydreaming about your passion while at your part-time job or skipping sleep to spend more time on your current obsession. Chances are, if you have a pulse, you already have a number of hobbies.

Hobbies come in all different types and are a great way to connect with others during your busy day-to-day life. You've got your run-of-the-mill hobbies like gaming and sports, but there's also a whole world of obscure hobbies out there to explore. Experts say it's important for adults to have hobbies in order to live a fulfilling life and this becomes increasingly more important as you age.

In addition to adding fulfillment to your life, hobbies are a great way to keep your mind sharp as you enter your golden years. Strategic games are popular around the world, with unique ones found on every continent. Mancala is one of the oldest games to still be played today and originated in Africa. It is a turn-based game where the players move seeds or stones around the pits on the game board.

If you're more energetic, you may prefer an active hobby to stay in shape. Sepak Takraw is a popular sport across Southeast Asia where the participants display an incredible amount of athleticism. The sport is similar to volleyball with an incredible twist; the players can't use their hands. Players leap to incredible heights while twisting and kicking the rattan ball. Check out a video online and prepare to be amazed!

Maybe you'd like a combination of brains and brawn in your hobby? Then Chessboxing may appeal to you. This sport is, just as it sounds, a combination of chess and boxing. Competitors go 11 rounds, alternating between the two disciplines until a winner emerges.

If you still haven't found your passion in life, fear not. Even the strangest of us can find a community of like-minded individuals.

Comprehension Check

Complete the Summary

Most people have __________ outside of their normal working lives. These interests are a great way to __________ with other people and build friendships. There are normal hobbies, but also more __________ hobbies to explore. Doctors and scientists say it is important for adults to have hobbies, and this becomes even more __________ as you __________. Hobbies can keep your mind __________, and can also help you stay in __________. Don't worry, everyone can find a __________ of people with similar interests.

True or False

1. There are not many obscure hobbies. (T / F)
2. Mancala is a recently created game. (T / F)
3. Sepak Takraw is popular in Southeast Asia. (T / F)
4. Players have to jump a lot when playing Sepak Takraw. (T / F)
5. Chessboxing combines mental and physical challenges. (T / F)

Let's Discuss

Would you rather try *Mancala, Sepak Takraw, or Chessboxing*? Why?

Phrasal Verbs

Check out - Look at, watch / *Appeal to* - Interest, cause satisfaction

1. Jimin: Have you ever been scuba diving?

   Nicole: No, swimming doesn't __________ me.
2. Mina: Hey, __________ that car over there. It's so ugly!

Building Communication

Obscure Hobbies

Pros	Cons

Paragraph Writing: Do you think you will have a hobby in your golden years? What will it be?

Grammar: Sentence Structure

When making sentences in English, there is a certain word order that you should use. If you know this order, then you can make sentences easily.

Subject	*Verb*	*Object (Indirect - Direct)*	*Manner/ Complement*	*Place*	*Time*
The boy	*smiled.*				
The girl	*looks*		*happy.*		
The kid	*threw*	*the textbook.*			
The teacher	*gave*	*the students homework.*			
His sister	*called*	*him*	*a genius.*		
They	*went*			*to school*	*yesterday.*

A. ***Unscramble the following sentences and place them in the correct order.***

1. mother / Jeremy / from / a / note / his / handed / me

____

2. passed / the / bottle / Kate / him / water

____

3. fed / dog / Larry / his / the / homework

____

B. ***Circle the incorrect words in the following sentences and rewrite the sentence in the correct order.***

1. The students English speak in the classroom.

____

2. She eats for breakfast carrots.

____

3. Sarah bought a cowboy hat her uncle.

____

Speaking Skill: Forming Responses

When forming responses to questions, it's best to use a complete sentence. With Yes/No Questions, first answer with *yes or no*, then use the same verb in your answer. Or, answer *yes or no*, then add additional information.

Yes/No Question	Answer
Do you like coffee?	Yes, I do. / No, I don't. / Yes, I like coffee.
Have you seen this video?	Yes, I have. / No, I haven't. / No, what is it?

With Wh- Questions, you should answer with the information that corresponds to your Wh- question word. You can find words that you need in order to answer the question in the question itself.

Wh- Question	Answer
Where are you meeting her?	I'm meeting her at the restaurant.
What time did he arrive?	He arrived at 3:00 p.m.

A. Practice. *Answer each question with a complete sentence.*

Question	Answer
Are you going shopping?	
How long was the movie?	
Did he tell you about it?	

B. Interview a partner. *Use the table below to ask each other about your last vacation and answer in complete sentences.*

→ *Ex. Where: I went to Jeju Island.*

Name	*Where*	*When*	*Who*	*What*	*How*
Me					

Wrap Up

1. Do you have any hobbies? If so, what are they?

2. How much time do you spend on your hobby?

3. How can you find a new hobby?

4. What hobbies are popular in your country?

5. Which hobbies are more popular with women? What about with men?

6. What do you think are the benefits of having a hobby?

7. What kind of hobbies do you think are best to have?

8. What do you think is the most a person should spend on their hobby?

9. What hobbies would you like to try if you didn't have to worry about time or money?

10. **Culture Talk: Which hobby from another country would you like to try?**

UNIT 02

It's a Celebration

Warm-up *Holiday Brainstorming*

Unique Korean Holidays

Write a list of unique Korean holidays

1. ____________________
2. ____________________
3. ____________________
4. ____________________
5. ____________________

Unique Foreign Holidays

Search for unique holidays from around the world

France: ____________________

Egypt: ____________________

Ireland: ____________________

USA: ____________________

Chile: ____________________

Vocabulary Focus

A. Definition Matching. ***Write the letter next to the correct word.***

______	1. celebrate (v.)	A.	a special ritual or behavior for an important event
______	2. sacred (adj.)	B.	merge; combine with another
______	3. commemorate (v.)	C.	related to religion
______	4. ceremony (n.)	D.	to have a social gathering to remember a special day or event
______	5. ancestors (n.)	E.	a person (older than grandparents) from whom a person is descended
______	6. secular (adj.)	F.	to remember and show respect for someone or something
______	7. integrate (v.)	G.	not connected or related to religion
______	8. religious (adj.)	H.	special because of a connection to a god or religion

B. Fill in the Blanks. ***Write the correct vocabulary word from above.***

1. This is a very old temple, so this land is considered __________.
2. Our __________ lived on this same land long ago, so we should be grateful to them.
3. In order to work efficiently, we need to __________ our plans with their plans.
4. Even though my family isn't __________, we still attend church on Christmas Day.
5. On Chuseok, some families hold a small __________ to honor their __________.
6. Some holidays are connected to religion, while others are completely __________.
7. Every year, I __________ my birthday with my close friends and family.
8. The statue was built to __________ the end of the war.

It's a Celebration

Which holiday do you like more: Halloween or Christmas? Thanksgiving or Chuseok? St. Patrick's Day or April Fool's Day?

Almost everyone loves holidays. "Holiday" comes from the words "holy" and "day". In the past, people celebrated most holidays because of religious reasons. Whether for Buddha's birthday or Christmas Day, people took a break from their daily routine to do something special.

While these days Christmas is a season for gifts and lights, its history is long and complicated. When the Roman Christians began conquering Europe, they wanted to spread their religion to their new subjects. In order to make Christianity easier to accept, they took existing regional holidays and integrated them into Christianity. These ancient holidays include Winter Solstice, Saturnalia, and Yule.

Other holidays commemorate special events such as the end of a war, or a country's independence. We show our respect for the memory of those who fought and died in battles. On holidays like Chuseok or Thanksgiving, people hold ceremonies to show gratitude to their ancestors. Even Halloween and Dia de los Muertos, which are now celebrated worldwide with costumes and parties, started out as festivals to commemorate dead ancestors.

While many holidays have a long tradition, others are more recent and celebrate non-religious people or events. For example, Mother's Day and Father's Day in the USA, or Parents' and Children's Day in Korea, celebrate our love and respect for our family members. Burns Night in Scotland and Bloomsday in Ireland celebrate the famous writers Robert Burns and James Joyce. These secular holidays focus on important people rather than religious figures.

More recently, people have created "unofficial" holidays for just about everything. Have you heard of Ice Cream for Breakfast Day? It was started by Florence Rappaport in New York in the 1960s, and now it's celebrated around the world. How about the Lopburi Monkey Buffet? On the last weekend in November, the people in the Thai village of Lopburi prepare a feast for the monkeys in the city. It includes fruit, nuts, meat, and even Coca-Cola! Even Black Day in Korea, which celebrates single people, is a recent and unique holiday! There are even holidays created by companies to make money. These are called "Hallmark" holidays.

If you could make up a new holiday, what would you celebrate?

Comprehension Check

Complete the Summary

Everybody loves __________. A long time ago we celebrated most holidays for __________ reasons. They are a great chance to take a __________ from our normal schedule and to do something __________. Other holidays __________ the past. Some examples are holidays for the end of a __________ or a country gaining __________. Not all holidays are for religious purposes. Some are __________ holidays and focus on important people instead of religious __________. Recently, people have created __________ holidays on a number of different days for all sorts of different reasons. Some holidays have even been created by companies in order to make money. We call these __________ holidays.

True or False

1. Traditional holidays never celebrated religious events. (T / F)
2. Christmas and Buddha's Birthday have religious roots. (T / F)
3. A holiday to recall the past may celebrate the end of a war. (T / F)
4. Parents' Day is an example of a recent holiday. (T / F)
5. Burns Night is an example of a religious holiday. (T / F)

Let's Discuss

What is your opinion of "Hallmark" holidays? Explain.

Phrasal Verbs:

Start out - Begin / *Make up* - Create, imagine

1. You need to __________ as an intern before you can work here.
2. This essay will require a lot of research. You can't just __________ random facts and examples.

Building Communication:

Hallmark Holidays

Hallmark is a famous greeting card company in the USA.
They make a lot of money from holidays when people buy cards for each other.
So any holiday that was created by a company to make money is called a "Hallmark holiday". Does your country have any Hallmark holidays?

Name	Who	When	How
Pepero Day	*Young people*	*November 11*	*Buy Pepero and give it to your date and friends*

Paragraph Writing: Try to create your own "Hallmark" holiday. Be sure to give it a name, explain why it is celebrated, when it is celebrated, and how it is celebrated.

Grammar: Forming Questions

When making questions in English, there are three rules you should remember.

1	Subject and verb change places.	You are the new employee. ➜ Are you the new employee?
2	Helping verb "do"- *Used with regular verbs*	You have an appointment. ➜ Do you have an appointment?
3	Question words go to the front of the sentence.*	He respects his boss a lot. ➜ Who does he respect a lot?
	**If the question word "who" is the subject, then use basic sentence structure.*	John got hired by the company. ➜ Who got hired by the company?
	Note: Prepositions, such as "with", "at", etc., or adjectives/adverbs will stay at the end of the sentence.	You play games with who. ➜ Who do you play games with?

A. ***Write questions using the following words.***

1. She/be/hungry

____

2. Your brother/play/video games

____

3. Who/go (past)/with you/to the store

____

B. ***Ask your partner questions to try to find two things in common.***

➜ *Example: What is your favorite color? What is your favorite food?*

1. ____
2. ____

Speaking Skill: Making Small Talk

Yes/No Questions often begin with the verbs Be, Do, and Have. These questions can be answered with Yes or No, plus additional information.
Wh- Questions begin with Who, What, Where, When, Why, Which, How. These questions require more information to answer.

Yes/No	"Wh-"
Do you like coffee?	What kind of coffee do you like?
Are you going to the concert?	Where is the concert?

Conversations often begin with a Yes/No Question, which is followed by one or more Wh- Questions.

A. ***Using what you just learned, practice writing questions below.***

Write a Yes/No Question.

___

Write a Wh- Question related to your Yes/No Questions.

___

B. Questions Game. ***One person in your group asks a question from the list above. But, instead of responding with an answer, you must respond with another question. For example:***

A: Do you want to play the questions game?

B: What kind of game is that?

C: Why do you want to play that game?

If you can't answer with a question, take too long, or your question is unrelated, you lose. Try to keep the conversation going for as long as you can.

Wrap Up

1. What is your favorite holiday? Why do you like that holiday?

____

2. What holidays are celebrated in your country?

____

3. What foods do you eat on holidays? Why do you eat those foods?

____

4. Do you spend holidays with your family or alone?

____

5. Do you give gifts on holidays? If so, what kinds of gifts do you give? If not, what kinds of gifts would you like to receive?

____

6. Do you think your country should have more or fewer holidays? Why?

____

7. Has celebrating holidays changed since you were a kid? If so, how?

____

8. Do think holidays are stressful or relaxing? Why?

____

9. What do you think about "Hallmark holidays"?

____

10. **Culture Talk: Which holiday that is celebrated in another country do you think is most interesting? Why?**

____

UNIT 03
What's Cookin'?

Warm-up *Daily Diet*

List the 5 foods that you eat most often:

1. ______________________________
2. ______________________________
3. ______________________________
4. ______________________________
5. ______________________________

Finish the following sentences:

My favorite snack is ______________

______________________________.

My favorite restaurant is ___________

______________________________.

I really hate ___________________

______________________________.

Vocabulary Focus

A. Definition Matching. ***Write the letter next to the correct word.***

______	1. vary (v.)		A. mention a different source for evidence
______	2. linked to (ph. v.)		B. causing an argument, controversial
______	3. processed (adj.)		C. moral, relating to good or bad behavior
______	4. contentious (adj.)		D. to differ in size, amount, or degree
______	5. fad (n.)		E. preserved using chemicals
______	6. ethical (adj.)		F. connected to
______	7. spectrum (n.)		G. trend, popular for a short time
______	8. cite (v.)		H. range of opinion

B. Fill in the Blanks. ***Write the correct vocabulary word from above.***

1. When you do research, you absolutely cannot forget to __________ your sources.
2. Even though this is a __________ social issue, I think we can all agree that something needs to change.
3. I really hate these new handbags. Everyone has them now! I think they are just a __________.
4. Doctors agree that consuming too much sugar is __________ type 2 diabetes.
5. White rice is so __________. There is not much nutritional value left.
6. I don't care where you are on the political __________; if you're a kind person, I have no problem with you.
7. I can't agree with your behavior. Cheating on the exam is simply not __________.
8. Eating habits across the world __________ quite a bit.

What's Cookin'?

What comes to mind when you think of the word "diet"? Maybe losing weight, or changing your appearance. Although the word diet often refers to losing weight, it can also mean "way of eating" or "one's typical eating habits". Diets around the world often vary as much as culture!

A country's food is often linked to their history, region, climate, and culture. For example, the Inuit people, who inhabit the cold Arctic regions of various countries, live mostly on fish and other animal products. Those who inhabit tropical climates, such as the Samoan people, traditionally ate more fruit, such as bananas and coconuts, as well as seafood.

These days, food is a contentious issue. People argue over what the "best" diet is. There are always fad diets when the issue is weight loss. These fad diets can be strange and extreme, such as the Cabbage Soup Diet, the Baby Food Diet, or the IU diet. There was even a fad diet called the Drinking Man's Diet, which only included meat and alcohol!

While new fad diets will always come and go, people also argue over which diet is best for our overall health. Let's take a look at some alternative diets.

One diet gaining popularity around the world is the vegan diet. Vegans eat no animal products at all, only plants. That means no meat, milk, butter, or even honey! Most people who take up a vegan diet do so because of the apparent health benefits, or for ethical reasons.

On the opposite side of the spectrum, some people have begun to follow a carnivore diet. Those on a carnivore diet eat only animal products, especially meat. A similar diet that also includes some plants is the Paleo diet, short for 'Paleolithic'. People on this diet usually cite the lifestyle of our distant ancestors who hunted wild animals and gathered wild fruits and vegetables.

While these diets might seem extreme, they have one thing in common: they cut out all processed or refined junk food. No cookies, cake, or candy! Do you think you could live without sweets?

One common idea about food is that it should be shared with others. Experts say that eating and enjoying meals together can improve mood, communication, and even productivity at school or work. So enjoy a meal with family or friends! Cheers!

Comprehension Check

Complete the Summary

The word diet often refers to losing __________, but it can also mean your way of eating or your __________ eating habits. Food is usually __________ to a country's history, region, climate, and culture. People in __________ climates typically have more fruit in their diets. Nowadays, there are a lot of __________ diets, such as the vegan diet or the carnivore diet. Vegans eat no __________ products, while people on the carnivore diet eat __________ animal products. These diets cut out all __________ foods.

True or False

1. Inuit people live in cold regions. (T / F)
2. Some people practice a vegan diet for ethical reasons. (T / F)
3. People on the paleo diet do not eat any animal products. (T / F)
4. Most vegans eat a lot of processed food. (T / F)
5. Eating meals with family can help improve your mood. (T / F)

Let's Discuss

Would you rather be on a carnivore or vegan diet? Why?

Phrasal Verbs:

Cut out - Stop doing something / *Take up* - Start something new

1. __________ excess sugars to maintain a healthy diet.
2. I'm bored. I'd like to __________ a new hobby, like playing the piano.

Building Communication

Fad Diets

Pros	Cons

Paragraph Writing: Do you think a healthy diet is more important than exercising? Explain.

Grammar: Descriptive Questions

Adjective questions are questions that you ask to learn more information about a certain noun/pronoun.

Which *(noun)* (do/does) + subject + verb?
You like which shirt? ➜ *Which shirt do you like?*

What (noun) (do/does) + subject + verb?
You listen to what kind of music? ➜ *What kind of music do you listen to?*

How (adjective) (do/does) + subject + verb?
It costs how much? ➜ *How much does it cost?*

Whose (noun) (do/does) + subject + verb?
This is whose book? ➜ *Whose book is this?*

A. ***Practice writing a question using the adjective question words.***

1. Which

____

2. How

____

3. Whose

____

B. ***Celebrity 20 questions. Below, write the name of a well-known person. Then let your group ask questions until they can guess your person (Example: Where were they born? How old are they?).***

Your celebrity: ______________________

Speaking Skill: Maintaining a Conversation

Follow-up Questions are used to get additional information about a certain topic. After someone has answered a question, you can ask extra questions about their answer to get more detail.

Question: What's your favorite food?
Answer: I'm a big fan of pizza.
Follow-up: Which pizza toppings do you like?
How often do you eat pizza?
Where is your favorite pizza restaurant?

Follow-up Questions are often Wh- Questions, but not always.
Yes/No Questions are also used. Using the example above, you might ask:

Have you eaten pizza recently?
Do you think pizza is better than samgyeopsal?
Did you eat a lot of pizza as a kid?

A. ***Write one possible Follow-up Question for each answer.***

1. Q: What is your favorite holiday?

A: I really love Halloween!

F: ______________________________

2. Q: Where do you want to travel for your next holiday?

A: I really want to visit Hong Kong.

F: ______________________________

B. ***Write one question similar to the questions in (A.) Then ask the question to your group. Each person should answer, and the others should ask at least one follow-up question.***

Wrap Up

1. Have you ever gone on a diet? If so, what kind of diet was it?

2. Why do people usually go on diets?

3. When do you think people should go on a diet?

4. What are some special diets that you have heard of? Have you tried any of them?

5. Is exercising an important part of a diet?

6. Is dieting a problem in your country? Why or why not?

7. Do you think the same diet works for everyone?

8. What are some problems with dieting?

9. Are there any popular diet trends in your country? What are they?

10. **Culture Talk: What good eating habits could people in your country learn from other countries to help them live a healthier life?**

UNIT 04

Pride and Prejudices

Warm-up *Gender Stereotypes*

What are 5 stereotypes for men?

Ex. Men love sports.

1. ______________________
2. ______________________
3. ______________________
4. ______________________
5. ______________________

What are 5 stereotypes for women?

Ex. Women love gossip.

1. ______________________
2. ______________________
3. ______________________
4. ______________________
5. ______________________

Vocabulary Focus

A. *Definition Matching. Write the letter next to the correct word.*

______	1. background (n.)	A.	hostility toward someone that is not based on reason or facts
______	2. to stereotype (v.)	B.	communicate with, contact
______	3. prejudice (n.)	C.	not on purpose
______	4. interact (v)	D.	a person's upbringing
______	5. based on (ph. v.)	E.	a group of people who have the same national, racial, or cultural origins
______	6. unintentionally (adv.)	F.	to make a generalization about a group of people
______	7. ethnicity (n.)	G.	knowing that something exists
______	8. aware (adj.)	H.	to use facts to make a decision

B. *Fill in the Blanks. Write the correct vocabulary word from above.*

1. You shouldn't __________ like that. Not all women like to cook.
2. Your opinion is not __________ any actual data or facts. I think you should reconsider this belief.
3. I was trying to get the teacher's attention, but I don't think he was even __________ of me.
4. He wanted to travel to Europe to learn more about his __________.
5. I __________ offended her today. It really was an accident.
6. Her __________ is a mystery to us. We don't know anything about her.
7. He had to overcome a lot of __________ simply because of the color of his skin.
8. He likes to stay in his room. He doesn't like to __________ with his family very much.

Pride and Prejudices

If you traveled back in time, you would see a very different world because of all the recent changes. Technology has developed very quickly within the last hundred years. The internet has helped the world become connected. Also, traveling between countries is now easier than ever. Anyone can get on a plane and be in another country in just a few hours. Cultures have changed a lot as a result of technology and people from different countries traveling around the globe. Unfortunately, not all of the effects of these changes have been positive.

Stereotyping is a problem that people face when meeting people from other cultures. Stereotypes are ideas we have about a group of people or people from a certain culture. It is normal for humans to organize things into groups. It helps us make sense of the world. However, this can have real effects on our interactions with people from different cultures. A stereotype could be thinking that people from Canada or Japan are all nice and polite or that people with a darker skin color are bad or scary. The problem with stereotypes is that they are not true for all people in a group, even stereotypes that you think are good.

Many people who decide to live or travel to another country will probably face some prejudice in their daily life. When they interact with the people of their new country, these people may already have an opinion about them. These opinions are almost never based on experience or fact and they are normally negative. Many things, small and large, have been done to groups of people because of prejudices. Some parents will not allow their children to marry someone from a different group. Some landlords will not rent to certain people because of their race or sexual orientation. Some companies will only hire women as secretaries. And sometimes, prejudices can lead to great tragedies in history like the Holocaust. It is very difficult for people to change their prejudices about people, but it is not impossible.

Sometimes prejudices can be hidden but unintentionally appear in the way we treat others based on our ideas about them. These are called microaggressions. In the United States, this may include asking someone who is not white where they are from because you do not think that they were born in the country based on their ethnicity. In Korea, this can be telling a non-Asian person that they are really good with chopsticks or asking if they can really eat spicy food. A good way to see if what you are saying or doing is a microaggression is to ask yourself, "Would I ask or do this to a person who is similar to me?" If the answer is no, you may want to stop doing or saying that thing.

Most people can agree that stereotypes and prejudice are not good things, but it is often difficult to admit that we hold some about other people. It is important to meet people from many different backgrounds so that we can become aware of the ideas we have about other people and change them.

Comprehension Check

Complete the Summary

The development of technology has made the world more __________. Additionally, going to other countries is now __________ than ever. One problem that can arise when meeting people from other cultures is __________. This is when we have generalized ideas about people from certain __________. It is important to meet people from other __________ in order to understand other cultures.

True or False

1. Technology has developed gradually over the last 100 years. (T / F)
2. Humans naturally organize things into groups. (T / F)
3. Most people will face prejudice at some point in their life. (T / F)
4. Prejudices can lead to tragedies. (T / F)
5. Most people agree that we need more prejudice and stereotypes. (T / F)

Let's Discuss

Think of some stereotypes that you have heard about other cultures.

Phrasal Verbs:

Come across - Find / *Own up* - Take responsibility for something

1. You need to __________ to your mistake.
2. I've never __________ anyone like him.

Building Communication

Traveling

Pros	Cons

Paragraph Writing: Write about a time when you experienced or witnessed prejudice. Write about what happened.

Grammar: Confirming Information

Negative sentences can be intimidating at first, but after you learn the rules, they're easy. They're also very useful if you do not know many words in English.

Basic Sentence

Be-verb (not)	*Subject + be-verb + not + adjective/noun.* I am hungry. ➜ I am not hungry.
Regular verb (do not)	*Subject + do not + regular verb.* I like eating dinner out. ➜ I do not like eating dinner out.

*Questions**

Be-verb (not)	*Be-verb + subject + not + adjective/noun?* You are not hungry. ➜ Are you not hungry?/ Aren't you hungry?
Regular verb (do not)	*Do + subject + not + verb?/Don't + subject + verb?* You don't like eating out. ➜ Do you not like eating out?/ Don't you like eating out?

**Negative questions are used to confirm information that you think is true.*

A. ***Change the sentences below to negative questions.***

1. He is going to Spain next week.

   ____

2. The plans look very interesting.

   ____

3. You are tired.

   ____

B. ***Write your own negative sentence below.***

____

Speaking Skill: Negative Questions

Negative Questions contain the word "not". These questions are usually used to confirm information that we think is true, or to express surprise and shock.

Normal Yes/No Question	Negative Question
Did you hear about Jeff?	Didn't you hear about Jeff?
Have you been to Jeju Island?	Haven't you been to Jeju Island?

We can also make Wh- Questions negative, to get different information.

Normal Wh- Question	Negative Question
What do you like about it?	What don't you like about it?
Why is she going?	Why isn't she going?

We also use negative questions in certain polite requests or suggestions.
Suggestion: *Why don't you* ask your friends for advice?
Request: *Wouldn't you* like to take some time off?

Practice

A. ***Turn each Question into a Negative Question.***

Normal Yes/No Question	Negative Question
Is your friend working at the cafe?	
Can you take the bus?	
Did you see the movie with your family?	

B. ***Change the underlined questions to negative questions.***

A: <u>Did you see the new Marvel movie</u>?

B: Yes, I saw it. <u>Did you hear about it?</u>

A: No, I didn't hear much about it. <u>Was it good?</u>

A: It was awesome. <u>Do you want to see it?</u>

Wrap Up

1. What are some stereotypes that other people have about people from your country?

2. What are some stereotypes that you have about people from other countries?

3. What are some stereotypes that you have about other groups of people in your own country?

4. Are there any advantages of stereotyping people? If so, what are they?

5. Have you ever treated someone differently because of a stereotype you have? If so, how?

6. Have you ever experienced prejudice? If so, give an example.

7. Why do you think people feel offended by stereotypes?

8. Can stereotypes be a good thing? If so, give an example.

9. How can stereotypes help or hurt you in different areas of your life? For example, getting a job or meeting new people?

10. **Culture Talk: What are some ways that we can improve the stereotypes/prejudices we have about people from other cultures?**

UNIT 05

Birds of a Feather Flock Together

Warm-up *Interesting & Uncommon Hobbies*

Ask your group members about their hobbies. Write 2 hobbies for each person.

Name: ______________

1. ______________________________

2. ______________________________

Name: ______________

1. ______________________________

2. ______________________________

Who has the most interesting hobby? What other strange or unique hobbies can you think of?

Name: ______________

1. ______________________________

2. ______________________________

Name: ______________

1. ______________________________

2. ______________________________

Vocabulary Focus

A. ***Definition Matching. Write the letter next to the correct word.***

______	1. subculture (n.)		A. many, more than one can count
______	2. mainstream (n.)/(adj.)		B. a person who really enjoys something
______	3. quirky (adj.)		C. a change or adjustment
______	4. rebellion (n.)		D. the beliefs and behaviors considered 'normal' by most people
______	5. conform (v.)		E. unique, strange in a good way
______	6. countless (adj.)		F. a group of people that follow an identity that is different from most people
______	7. modification (n.)		G. a group that fights against something
______	8. enthusiast (n)		H. to follow and agree with the majority

B. ***Fill in the Blanks. Write the correct vocabulary word from above.***

1. Wow! You bought tickets to the concert? I never knew you were such a K-Pop __________!
2. There are __________ ways to make money online these days.
3. She doesn't have normal hobbies. Most of her friends describe her as __________.
4. The old house is a fixer-upper; it needs a few minor __________ before anyone can live there.
5. Well, if you enjoy dressing like a zombie, that's fine. I guess there is a __________ for everyone these days.
6. My favorite band used to be small, but they became __________. Now everyone loves them and their concert tickets are so expensive.
7. The citizens protested against the government all summer, but the __________ was finally crushed by police.
8. Most people __________ to the rules of society. But not me; I go my own way.

Birds of a Feather Flock Together

Do you think you're an animal trapped in a human body? Do you think feeling sick is cute? If so, you might want to join a subculture. A subculture is a group of people that have a different identity than the mainstream culture. They often express their own identity through unique fashion, beliefs, behaviors, or even sexuality and body modification. At first, subcultures can appear unusual, quirky, or even strange. Let's take a closer look.

In the United States, hippies and bikers were two famous subcultures. Although neither group took part in the mainstream culture, they stood for different things. Hippies advocated peace and love, while the bikers advocated freedom, loyalty and not conforming to society. Another famous subculture, 'punk', began in the US and UK in the mid-1970s. The punk scene, like most subcultures, was characterized by rebellion against authority and freedom of expression through fashion and body art. Punk, in particular, rebelled against popular trends in music, and instead celebrated a crazy, energetic performance.

Hip hop music also began as a subculture. In the late 1970s in New York City, hip hop emerged as an expression of urban, African-American culture through music, art, language, fashion and style. Now, hip hop music has spread to a global audience.

There are countless subcultures around the world. For example, in Japan, there is a subculture called *yami-kawaii*, which means "sick-cute". Girls wear pink and purple bandages and clothing depicting knives, syringes, and pills. Most are not really sick, they just enjoy the fashion. In Africa, a subcultural movement known as "La Sape" is a group of African men, known as "sapeurs", who dress in expensive suits and extravagant fashion. Although the men may not be rich, they wear the clothes of a gentleman to rebel against the reputation of Africa as a poor continent.

A subculture can also simply be those who share an uncommon interest. With the development of the internet, people from around the world can connect to talk about and share their unusual preferences. From train or elevator enthusiasts, to people who believe they are animals or spirits trapped in a human body ('furries' or 'otherkin'), the internet allows us to find others who share our unique interests and beliefs.

Parents are often uneasy about their children joining subcultures. They may fear the unknown or want to protect their children from bullying. Similarly, young people on the outside of a subculture may misunderstand or look down on those participating in it.

Comprehension Check

Complete the Summary

A group of people with a different __________ to the __________ culture can be called a __________. Two famous subcultures in the United States were the __________ and __________. The hippies were all about __________ and __________. Hip hop is another subculture that comes from __________ culture. In Japan, *yami kawaii* girls wear clothes with pictures of __________, __________, and __________. In Africa, sapeurs wear __________ suits to __________ against a common misunderstanding. The __________ has allowed people from around the world to __________ and share their unusual preferences.

True or False

1. Hip hop began in New York City in the late 1990s. (T / F)
2. Punk began in the US and the UK in the early 1980s. (T / F)
3. We can share unique interests online. (T / F)
4. Hip hop music originated in rural areas. (T / F)
5. The hippies stood for peace and love. (T / F)

Let's Discuss

Has the internet had a positive or negative effect on subcultures?

Phrasal Verbs:

Take part in - Participate in / *Stand for* - Endure, Tolerate

1. I can't believe you let your boss talk to you like that! I would never __________ that.
2. We need more people to __________ this survey.

Building Communication

Read the following conversation to complete the writing below.

Paragraph Writing: *Read the conversation above. What is your opinion about "hon-bap" culture?*

Grammar: Countable Nouns

Nouns in English can be "countable" or "uncountable". This can affect how they are used in a sentence.

Countable nouns are things that we can count.

- They have singular and plural forms.
  ➜ One mouse (singular) - two mice (plural)
- If they are singular, then they are preceded by articles (a/an or the).
  ➜ A girl ran across the street. (O) ➜ A two girls ran across the street. (X)

Uncountable nouns are things that cannot be counted. They are usually abstract nouns* and are often used with counters.

- They are not preceded by articles.
  ➜ Watch your step! Water is all over the floor.
- They are used together with counters or quantity words like *a lot*, *a little*, *some*, and *much*.
  ➜ Let me give you some advice.

*Abstract nouns are usually ideas or feelings, things made of tiny parts (rice, sand, etc.), liquids and gases (air, milk, etc.), minerals (gold, silver, etc.), and specific people or places.

A. ***Circle the correct answer below. If you do not need to add a word, circle the "X".***

1. **(A/An/X)** Busan is a big city.
2. **(A/An/X)** ant is a diligent insect.
3. **(A/An/X)** Carol is a nurse.
4. **(A/An/X)** gold is expensive.
5. **(A/An/X)** milk spilled on the counter.
6. **(A/An/X)** dish broke on the kitchen floor.

Speaking Skill: Introducing Topics

You can introduce new topics using either a question or a statement. Here are a few expressions to naturally introduce a new topic.

Question	Statement
Did you hear/see that ________?	I heard/saw that ________.
Did you hear about ________?	I heard about ________.
Did you see ________?	I saw ________.

*If your question or statement contains "that", it should be followed by a complete sentence. If it does not contain "that", it should be followed by a noun or adjective+ noun. For example:

Ji-eun got married.

Question	Statement
Did you hear that Ji-eun got married?	I heard/saw that Ji-eun got married.
Did you hear about Ji-eun's wedding?	I heard about Ji-eun's wedding.
Did you see Ji-eun's wedding pictures?	I saw Ji-eun's wedding pictures.

Practice

A. ***Write one question and one statement introducing each topic.***

1. New Topic: There is a new restaurant near school.

Question: ________________

Statement: ________________

2. New Topic: Eunhee's new boyfriend.

Question: ________________

Statement: ________________

B. *Write down 3 new topics you'd like to introduce to your team or classmates. These can be topics from school, the news, or from your personal life. Have a discussion with your team about these topics. Try to continue the conversation about one topic for 2 minutes using **Follow-up Questions**.*

Wrap Up

1. Do you know of any popular subcultures in your country?

   ____

2. Which subculture is the most unusual to you? Explain why.

   ____

3. Why do people join subcultures?

   ____

4. What do subcultures give people that mainstream culture can't?

   ____

5. Do you think it's better to be a part of mainstream culture only or to join a subculture?

   ____

6. What do older people usually think about modern subcultures? Explain.

   ____

7. What are the advantages and disadvantages of being part of a subculture?

   ____

8. Which subculture would you rather join: *yami kawaii* or *la sape style*? Why?

   ____

9. If you could make a new subculture about your interest, which interest would you choose? How would you express your subculture's identity?

   ____

10. **Culture Talk: Is there a subculture in another country you wish would come to your country?**

    ____

UNIT 06

A Whole New (Digital) World

Warm-up *Online Communities*

List the 5 websites you visit most often:

1. ______________________
2. ______________________
3. ______________________
4. ______________________
5. ______________________

What are 3 popular online communities?

____

Are you a part of any online communities?

____

Do you have any online friends?

____

Vocabulary Focus

A. Definition Matching. ***Write the letter next to the correct word.***

______	1. triggered (v.)		A. an estimate of a future situation; forecast
______	2. proliferation (n.)		B. rapid increase in numbers
______	3. mind-boggling (adj.)		C. things that rouse activity in someone
______	4. subsequent (adj.)		D. exceed; be greater than
______	5. projection (n.)		E. overwhelming; startling
______	6. surpass (v.)		F. lacking interest or excitement; dull
______	7. mundane (adj.)		G. caused an event to happen or exist
______	8. stimuli (n.)		H. coming after something; following

B. Fill in the Blanks. ***Write the correct vocabulary word from above.***

1. __________ editions of the book will be released next year.
2. He won the championship a __________ six times in his career.
3. She doesn't enjoy the __________ tasks required for her job.
4. The terrible incident __________ a riot in the streets.
5. The past few years have seen a __________ of streaming services.
6. Concert attendance is expected to __________ last year's record.
7. The children responded to auditory __________.
8. The analyst's __________ is that the market will continue on an upward trend.

A Whole New (Digital) World

Every new generation seems to be spending more and more time online with the proliferation of Internet culture into all aspects of life. This has given rise to a mind-boggling number of Internet subcultures and communities. Many of these communities seem strange or even unfathomable to all the grandparents out there, but the younger generation knows these communities will never die down.

One insanely popular community is the world of gaming and game streaming. Game streaming is when a gamer films him or herself while playing a video game. This can be entertaining for fans of any particular game and can also teach them techniques and strategies to improve when playing on their own. The streaming of video games started to gain popularity around 2010 with games like *League of Legends*, and has been growing rapidly every subsequent year. Sites like *Twitch* and *afreecaTV*, along with eSports champions pocketing large sums of money for winning gaming tournaments, have taken this craze to new heights. Projections show that this trend will only continue to grow in the years to come. Some experts even predict that esports could surpass traditional sports in terms of viewership in the future.

Many people believe that the expansion of the Internet and our wired world have made it more difficult for young people to fall asleep. If you find yourself with this problem, ASMR could be the answer to your woes. ASMR, or autonomous sensory meridian response, helps people relax and fall asleep. It is described as using auditory and visual stimuli to create a tingling sensation on the skin that starts at the scalp and moves down your spine. This can be triggered through all sorts of mundane tasks, such as a person whispering or turning the pages of a book over and over again. To some this trend seems strange, but others swear by its effectiveness.

Another interesting development as a result of sites like *YouTube* is the rise of product reviewers with large followings. Product reviewers film themselves opening different products and sharing their first impressions as well as giving in-depth commentary on the quality of any product you can think of. Some of the most successful reviewers are very young and review different toys for children. On the other hand, some reviewers are very technical and provide detailed information about a wide range of high-tech products, which can help you figure out if a big purchase is right for you.

As you can see, there's a community out there for any interest you may have.

Comprehension Check

Complete the Summary

Over the last decade, the amount of __________ spent online has __________ considerably for most people. Nowadays, there are a mind-boggling __________ of subcultures online. One popular community is the world of gaming and game __________. Fans of game streamers can learn new techniques and __________ when watching a stream. Some streamers are even __________ these days. This trend will likely continue to __________ in the following years. Some even think that esports could __________ traditional sports in the future. ASMR is another trend that helps people __________ and fall __________. ASMR creates a tingling __________ for many people which helps them relax. Another interesting trend is __________ products. Product reviewers __________ themselves opening products and giving their __________.

True or False

1. Game streaming became popular in 2001. (T / F)
2. The top esports competitors can make a lot of money. (T / F)
3. Auditory and visual stimuli are used in ASMR. (T / F)
4. All product reviewers are adults. (T / F)
5. There are online communities out there for all different interests. (T / F)

Phrasal Verbs:

Die down - Become less popular, disappear / *Figure out* - Solve

1. I'm really struggling in Mr. Park's class. I can't __________ any of the homework problems.
2. She's so passionate about studying. Her enthusiasm will never __________.

Building Communication

Internet Subcultures

Pros	Cons

Paragraph Writing: Do you think online product review videos are beneficial to watch before buying something? Explain why or why not.

Grammar: Participles

Participles are verbs that are used as other parts of speech.

Present participles are always made by adding "-ing" to the verb root. Past participles are usually made by adding "-ed" to the verb root. However, some words have irregular past participle forms, so be careful.

Present Participles	*Past Participles*
*similar to active verbs	*have passive meanings
→ The falling leaves are so beautiful.	→ The fallen leaves are like a red and orange ocean.
→ The movie was interesting.	→ She was interested in the movie

A. ***Complete the sentences below with the correct participle form of the verb.***

1. Kimiko recommended this __________ book. She was __________ by the author's talent with words. (*interest/amaze*)
2. Jean felt so __________ after taking a trip to the mountains. (*relax*)
3. The __________ water was too hot to drink. (*boil*)

B. **Participle Madlib.** ***First, fill in the list on the left with present or past participles without looking at the paragraph. Then, with a partner, practice reading your paragraph to see what interesting paragraphs you made.***

1. ________________ (*present*)
2. ________________ (*present*)
3. ________________ (*past*)
4. ________________ (*present*)

There was a _(1)_ girl who loved playing games. One day, she found a _(2)_ game online and decided to play it. After playing it, she felt very _(3)_. So she shared that game with her _(4)_ friends online.

Speaking Skill: Asking For & Giving Opinions

Asking for and giving your opinion is an essential conversation skill.

Asking for	Giving
What do you think about ___________?	I think ___________________________.
How do you feel about ____________?	I feel that ________________________.
What are your thoughts on _________?	I think ___________________________.
What's your opinion on ____________?	In my opinion, ____________________.

Giving your opinion is fine, but it will be stronger if followed by a reason.

Asking for: How do you feel about the fine dust problem in Korea?

Giving: I feel that it's a serious problem *because* many people develop health problems and die each year.

A. ***With your partner/team, make a list of topics to ask others' opinions on.***

Fine Dust		
Pizza		
English class		
Skiing		

B. ***Using the list of topics you created, interview your classmates to discover their opinions on various topics. Ask each student about 2 or 3 topics, then switch to a new person.***

Topic	*Name*	*Opinion*

Wrap Up

1. How much time do you spend on the internet each day?

2. What do you usually do on the internet?

3. Are you a part of any online groups or communities? If so, what are they?

4. What are some popular communities on the internet in your country?

5. What are some examples of communities that you can find online but they are difficult to find in person?

6. Has an internet community influenced your daily offline life? If so, how?

7. Do you think being a part of an offline community is better than being a part of an online community?

8. Do you watch any game streamers? What games do you watch? Why?

9. What do people in your country think about being a part of online communities?

10. **Culture Talk: Have you heard of an interesting online community in another country?**

UNIT 07

Getting on up There in Years

Warm-up *Coffin Catastrophe*

Think about the possession you love the most. Got it?

Now imagine you are buried in a coffin designed after that object. Describe it without using that word:

____

____

____

____

____

Now read your description to your team and see if they can guess!

Draw a picture of your coffin here:

Vocabulary Focus

A. Definition Matching. ***Write the letter next to the correct word.***

_______	1. to age (v.)	A. the process of burying the dead
_______	2. elderly (n.) / (adj.)	B. traditional beliefs or behaviors of a culture
_______	3. funeral (n.)	C. life after death
_______	4. customs (n.)	D. a way to refer to the dead person(s)
_______	5. to honor (v.)	E. to grow old; to become mature
_______	6. afterlife (n.)	F. to show deep respect for someone or something
_______	7. the deceased (n.)	G. to honor someone after they die, usually by attending their funeral
_______	8. to pay respect (ph. v.)	H. a way to refer to old people as a group

B. Fill in the Blanks. ***Write the correct vocabulary word from above.***

1. People of various religions believe in an ___________.
2. The concert is very expensive but there is a discount for the ___________.
3. I can't believe she's 50 years old. She has ___________ so well.
4. We ___________ our parents and grandparents on this holiday every year.
5. The family of ___________ will arrive soon to mourn their loss.
6. The country is changing rapidly, but local ___________ will never go away.
7. The ___________ will be held at our church this Saturday.
8. This statue is here ___________ to all the victims of this terrible tragedy.

Getting on Up There in Years

Humans have worried about aging and death for a long time. Growing old and dying are things that we all do, however, they are not done the same way around the world.

In Confucian countries, like Korea, Japan, or China, the elderly should be respected and taken care of by the youth. In many Western countries like the United States, getting older is usually seen as scary. Koshin Paley Ellison, a Buddhist monk, said of Americans, "People themselves when they're aging feel that there's something wrong with them and they're losing value." However, in many Native American cultures, getting old is seen as important because the elders of a tribe pass down wisdom to the younger generations.

The ways that cultures think about death are also diverse. Author Dr. Ronald K. Barrett said that death is thought of as part of the "natural rhythm of life" in some African-American communities and funerals can often be lively events. The Ga-Adangbe people of Ghana believe there is an afterlife after they die, and prepare for the journey with coffins designed after what the person was interested in when they were alive. In Japan, children are taught about death from a young age and it is considered a natural part of life that we must accept. Interestingly, the Urhobo of Nigeria have a special way of thinking about death. Although they are Christian, they believe in witchcraft. They also believe there are good deaths and bad deaths. To have a good death, you must live past the age of 70 because dying young is seen as immoral. If you have a bad death, then you are not given a proper funeral.

Naturally, since cultures think about aging and dying in different ways, the customs and traditions are also varied. In Sweden, they do *dostadning*, or "death cleaning", which is getting rid of unnecessary belongings so that when they die, their family is not burdened. Koreans honor their ancestors by preparing special food and doing ceremonies, called *charye* and *seongmyo*, during the Lunar New Year and *Chuseok*. Similar to Korea, Mexico also has a day to pay respect to their ancestors called *Dia de los Muertos*. On this day, they believe their loved ones visit Earth, so they set up tables, known as *ofrendas*, with pictures of their family members, prepare their favorite foods, and have a happy celebration. In some Western countries, they have wakes. Before the funeral, people will gather to express their feelings and emotions and tell stories about the deceased.

As you see, we can learn a lot from other cultures about how to age and die. So, which way seems most interesting to you? Have you changed how you think about death?

Comprehension Check

Complete the Summary

Humans have worried about death and __________ for a long time. There are many __________ ways to think about getting older. In __________ countries, senior citizens should be respected and taken __________ of by the youth. In many __________ countries, getting older is considered scary and people feel like they are losing value. In Native American communities, getting older is important because the elders of the tribe pass down __________ to the younger generations. As different cultures have diverse thoughts about death, there are different traditions and __________ as well.

True or False

1. Thinking and stressing about aging is a recent phenomenon. (T / F)
2. Funerals in African-American communities are always somber events. (T / F)
3. Children in Japan are taught about death from a young age. (T / F)
4. The Urhobo of Nigeria are Christian. (T / F)
5. "Death cleaning" is practiced in Sweden. (T / F)

Let's Discuss

Can you think of any other traditions related to aging?

Phrasal Verbs:

Passed away - Died / *Passed down* - Given to the next generation

1. I'm really sad. My dog __________ last night.
2. This necklace was __________ from my great grandmother.

Building Communication

Getting Older

Pros	Cons

Paragraph Writing: Do you think it's important to honor your ancestors? Why?

Grammar: Comparatives and Superlatives

Use comparatives to compare one quality between two things.

Adjective (1 syllable/ ends in -y)	+er	than

big ➜ Elephants are bigger than lions.
hairy ➜ Lions are hairier than elephants.

more	*Adjective* (2+ syllables)	than

beautiful ➜ Fall is more beautiful than spring.

When you compare one quality between three or more things, then you use the superlative form. It is similar to the comparative form.

the	*Adjective* (1 syllable/ ends in -y)	+est	noun

➜ Cheetahs are the fastest animal in the world.

the	most / least	*Adjective* (2+ syllables)	noun

➜ Blue diamonds are the most expensive stones in the world.

A. Grammar Practice. ***Fill in the blanks using the adjectives in parentheses.***

1. My kitten is ______________________ her cat. (cute)
2. The wedding was ______________________ day of her life. (happy)
3. Having fun is ______________________ winning the game. (important)
4. Losing your phone is ______________________ thing ever! (stressful)
5. I learned how to drive ______________________ my brothers. (early)

B. ***Celebrity Superlatives. With your partner/group, ask and answer who you think is the most beautiful/talented/etc. celebrity. Use the adjectives listed.***

➜ Gongyu is the most handsome actor. IU is the most beautiful singer.

talented funny beautiful nice

Speaking Skill: Agreeing & Disagreeing

Expressions of agreement or disagreement usually follow an opinion or statement. While "I agree" and "I disagree" are correct, below are additional phrases.

Agree	Disagree
I couldn't agree more.	I completely disagree.
I totally agree.	I have to disagree.
I'm with you on that.	I don't think so.
I see your point.	I don't understand where you're coming from.

The expressions at the top are stronger, while those below are weaker. Expressions of agreement and disagreement are commonly paired with reasons.

A. ***Read each opinion and write one expression of agreement or disagreement. Follow each expression with a reason.***

Opinion: Lying is okay sometimes.

____

Opinion: Drinking alcohol is good for your health.

____

B. ***Discuss the following opinions with your group. Each student should answer with an expression of agreement or disagreement, followed by a reason.***

Money is more important than love

Pizza is better than tteokbokki

HomePlus is better than Emart

Wrap Up

1. How often do you think about death?

2. How do people from your country think about death?

3. Why do you think people are afraid of dying?

4. Would you rather attend a lively or somber funeral? Why?

5. What are funerals like in your country?

6. What do you think happens after you die?

7. Do you like the idea of designing a coffin based on your interests?

8. What would your coffin look like?

9. If you could choose when and how you would die, would you?

10. **Culture Talk: Do you think people from your country could improve the way they think about death? How?**

UNIT 08

Making the Grade

Warm-up *Private Academies*

Did you attend a private academy (hagwon)?

Pros:	Cons:
______________________	______________________
______________________	______________________
______________________	______________________
______________________	______________________

Vocabulary Focus

A. Definition Matching. ***Write the letter next to the correct word.***

_______	1. naturally (adv.)		A. wanting to do something very much
_______	2. to observe (v.)		B. to be present at an event
_______	3. eager (adj.)		C. a long period of time
_______	4. to attend (v.)		D. without help or intervention
_______	5. to approach (v.)		E. required by laws or rules
_______	6. long run (n.)		F. to deal with something in a certain way
_______	7. mandatory (adj.)		G. to notice, perceive, or watch
_______	8. allowed (v.)		H. permitted to do something

B. Fill in the Blanks. ***Write the correct vocabulary word from above.***

1. Bikes are not __________ on this sidewalk.
2. He can't wait to graduate. He's so __________ to start working.
3. There is a training meeting on Saturday. Attendance is __________.
4. These plants grow __________ in my yard.
5. These scientists __________ monkeys in order to understand their habits.
6. Will you __________ the concert this Friday?
7. Most people study at home but he takes a different __________.
8. It may seem strange but it will be beneficial in the __________.

Making the Grade

From the moment we are born, we are absorbing information without trying. When we are young, we do it naturally by observing our parents or the people around us. In most countries, when children turn around 6-years-old, they start to go to school. From then on, we start to learn in a structured way. However, education and learning are not the same around the world.

Each culture has a different way to approach learning. Some countries, especially many in Asia, approach it through rote memorization. That is, students learn by listening to the teacher and studying notes again and again until they memorize them. Cramming is a type of rote memorization and is great to help students recall information quickly for taking tests, but may not be beneficial for long-term knowledge. On the other hand, some cultures prefer to develop students' critical thinking skills. This type of learning focuses on students working with the subject in a way that makes them think and try to understand the subject more deeply. Many researchers say that it may be more beneficial in the long run.

Who can and can't go to school is also different depending on where you're from. In some places, like South Korea or Canada, almost all kids are able to go to school. In fact, school is mandatory in many countries. However, in some places around the world, school is only something for those who luck out. In many countries, parents do not have enough money to send their kids to school. Sometimes, they have to send their kids to work instead, but many kids in those countries dream of going to school to be able to have a better life. Also, in some countries, girls are not allowed to go to school. Malala Yousafzai is a girl from Pakistan who fought for the right to attend school for herself and other girls in her country. She nearly ended up being killed by the Taliban for speaking out.

The way schools look can also be different around the world. In some poorer countries, students will gather outside by a tree or at a park, bringing old notebooks to listen to an adult teach them. Some countries have small buildings without air conditioning, books, or even pencils, but they do have eager students who want to learn. In Bangladesh, the school comes to the kids. They have boat schools because there are so many floods. Thanks to technology, some students don't need to leave their house to go to school. They go to school online.

Education is given easily to some students, but some kids around the world are not so lucky. It can be inspiring to think about the places around the world where it is difficult for people to get an education but still try.

Comprehension Check

Complete the Summary

When we are young, we absorb information by __________ the world around us. Children start to learn in a __________ way when they start school. Each culture has a different __________ to learning. For example, rote memorization is more common in __________ countries. School is mandatory in most countries, but there are some places where attending school is only for those who are __________. There are even countries where girls are not __________ to go to school. Nowadays, some students do not even need to go to a brick and mortar school. They can attend classes __________ in the comfort of their home.

True or False

1. We start absorbing information as soon as we are born. (T / F)
2. Every culture approaches learning in the same way. (T / F)
3. There are some boat schools in Bangladesh. (T / F)
4. Cramming is a type of deep learning. (T / F)
5. Malala Yousafzai fought for the right for girls to attend school. (T / F)

Let's Discuss

Do you prefer deep learning or rote memorization? Why?

Phrasal Verbs:

End up - To finally be in a particular place or situation / *Luck out* - To be lucky

1. If you don't start working hard, you'll __________ without a job.
2. The Doosan Bears really __________ last night. They shouldn't have won that game.

Building Communication

Online Schools

Online schools are beneficial because:

Online schools are harmful because:

Paragraph Writing: What do you think are the most important skills for students of the future generation? Why?

Grammar: Conjunctions

Conjunctions are words that are used to join two parts of a sentence or two different sentences. There are three types:

1. Coordinating-join together words, phrases, or two independent clauses. There are seven: "For", "And", "Nor", "But", "Or", "Yet", and "So". You can easily remember them by thinking of the acronym FANBOYS.
   → *Sean doesn't like chocolate or strawberries.*
   → *I want to go see a movie this weekend, but I am too busy to go.*
2. Subordinating-join together an independent clause and a dependent clause. Some of the most common ones are: "after", "because", "before", "if", "when", and "since".
   → *When I was young, I couldn't swim.*
   → *The baby is crying because she is hungry.*
3. Correlative-come in pairs and work together to show the relationship between two parts of the sentence. Some correlative conjunctions include "both/and", "either/or", "not/but", and "not only/but also".
   → *I would like a piece of both the chocolate and the vanilla cake.*
   → *She is not only beautiful but also smart.*

A. ***Complete the sentences using the correct conjunction.***

1. Mom said we had to wait ___________ she got back from work.
2. ___________ Kai worked out at the gym, she went home to eat lunch.
3. The baby is a really picky eater. He doesn't like to eat green vegetables ___________ most fruits. It makes his mom worry about his health.
4. Zack couldn't decide which dessert to order. He wanted to eat ___________ the angel cake ___________ red velvet cake.
5. Noor couldn't focus on her work ___________ she took a walk to help clear her mind.

B. ***On another piece of paper, try to make the longest sentence that you can by using conjunctions. Make sure your sentence is grammatically correct.***

Speaking Skill: Expressing Reasons

The most common way to express a reason is to use the word because. However, we can also use the words since, as, so, because of and due to.
When expressing reasons, think about two things: reason and result.

Because, Since, As, So

With "because, since, and as", the result comes before the reason.

Reason: I ate too much chicken.

Result: I feel sick.

Sentence: I feel sick because/since/as I ate too much chicken.

With "so", the reason comes before the result.

Sentence: I ate too much chicken so I feel sick.

Because of, Due to

With "because of" and "due to", the reason isn't a full sentence, just a noun.

Reason: The snowstorm.

Result: School was canceled.

Sentence: School was canceled because of/due to the snowstorm.

A. ***Read each reason and result and write the correct answer.***

1. Reason: I didn't eat breakfast. / Result: I'm really hungry.

Sentence: ______________________________

2. Reason: My friend's wedding. / Result: I can't hang out on Saturday.

Sentence: ______________________________

B. **"WHY?"** ***Using Wh- words and negative questions, write 3 more questions using "why." Then ask your partner or team members each question.***

Why can't you hang out this weekend?

Why didn't you call me back?

1. ______________________________

2. ______________________________

3. ______________________________

Wrap Up

1. Do you like learning new things? Why or why not?

2. What was the best learning experience you ever had?

3. Do you think that people stop learning after they leave school?

4. What are some ways to make learning fun?

5. Do you think you are born naturally smart or is it something you can train?

6. Do you think school is a waste of time? How about learning new things?

7. How old do you think is too old to learn something new?

8. Do you learn best by listening or doing?

9. Why do you think some people are better at learning new things compared to other people?

10. **Culture Talk: How would you like your country to change its education system to be like other countries?**

UNIT 09

The Language Heard 'Round the World

Warm-up *Traveling with English*

Write the foreign countries you've traveled to:	When did you use English in that country? In which places or situations?
____________________	____________________
____________________	____________________
____________________	____________________
____________________	____________________
____________________	____________________

Vocabulary Focus

A. Definition Matching. ***Write the letter next to the correct word.***

______	1. adapt (v.)	A. extra space to move or negotiate
______	2. cooperation (n.)	B. a part or feature of something
______	3. abstract (adj.)	C. existing as an idea, but not a physical object
______	4. aspect (n.)	D. not from to a certain place
______	5. associate (v.)	E. change for a new use
______	6. non-native (adj.)/(n.)	F. working together
______	7. native (adj.)/(n.)	G. to connect in your mind
______	8. wiggle room (n.)	H. born in a certain place

B. Fill in the Blanks. ***Write the correct vocabulary word from above.***

1. My friend is a __________ Hawaiian. She was born and raised there.
2. I need to write down my idea for the essay. It's still too __________.
3. Although our travel schedule is tight, we still have some __________. We can fit one or two more activities.
4. A lack of money is only one __________ of the problem. There's a lot more we need to understand.
5. I always __________ that cafe with my ex-girlfriend. We went there all the time.
6. Jeju horses are native to Korea. But most other horses are __________.
7. Social media is a big part of our lives, so businesses everywhere have to __________ and change with the times.
8. __________ between various governments makes global trade possible.

The Language Heard 'Round the World

We've all heard it before: "English is the global language." What comes to mind when you think of the word "global"? You might think about business, international trade, or the global economy. You might think about communication and cooperation between governments. But these ideas are a little abstract. What does the word global mean in your life?

For example, imagine you are traveling alone in France. You want to buy coffee at a small cafe near the Eiffel Tower, but you're nervous because you don't speak French. The staff at the cafe probably don't speak your native language either. However, if you both can speak even a little English, you'll be able to get your coffee. Now, imagine you are on a train in India. You woke up early and you're traveling to see the Taj Mahal. A young Indian boy is staring at you from across the train. Suddenly, he comes over, smiles and asks a question in English. Can you answer him? If you speak English well, you could get to know more people and experience your travels in a deeper way.

There is another aspect to the meaning of "global language" as well. While we might associate English with countries like the USA, England or Australia, the truth is that there are far more people who speak English as a second language (non-native speakers) than people who speak it as a first language (native speakers). This means that in many situations, when you use English, you'll be talking to another non-native speaker.

The English language has evolved over time, so each country has its own unique version of English. There are countless 'Englishes': Chinese English, Singaporean English, Indian English and even Korean English! Each country takes standard English and adds its own flavor and culture, which creates new and unique words and uses. You will meet and talk to people using all different versions of English, so never worry about messing up! When speaking English, sharing ideas is more important than perfect grammar.

Another interesting result of English being everywhere, or "global", is that English is constantly changing and adapting. While there are certain grammar rules we follow to make communication easier, there is a lot of wiggle room. You can adapt English to meet your needs!

English is a tool, one of many tools you can use in your life. So set off into the world and make English yours!

Comprehension Check

Complete the Summary

Some people describe English as the ___________ language. Learning a common language can help you experience your travels in a ___________ way. In fact, a lot more people around the world speak English as a ___________ language than as a ___________ language. This means when you use English, you will often be speaking with another ___________ speaker. Every country has a unique ___________ of English. Additionally, English is always changing and ___________.

True or False

1. English is considered the global language by many people. (T / F)
2. Learning English is not helpful when traveling. (T / F)
3. Most people around the world speak English as a first language. (T / F)
4. Many countries have their own unique version of English. (T / F)
5. The English language is always changing. (T / F)

Let's Discuss

Think of two "Konglish" words. Share them with the class.

Phrasal Verbs:

Set off - Leave / *Mess up* - Make a mistake

1. I didn't study at all, so I really ___________ on the test.
2. We need to have our bags packed before we ___________ on the trip.

Building Communication

The English Language

Pros	Cons

Paragraph Writing: Have you ever had to use English when traveling? Explain.

Grammar: Relative Clauses

Relative clauses give more information about a noun. They start with a pronoun such as who, that, which, whose, and whom. They are followed by a verb and noun/adjective.

Example: Children who hate chocolate are rare.

The extra information provided by relative clauses can define something (defining clause) or provide unnecessary, but interesting, information (non-defining clause).

- Non-defining clauses are surrounded by commas and can be removed from the sentence without changing the meaning of the sentence.

Example:

(Defining Clause) My brother who works for Samsung got a new car. (this implies multiple brothers)

(Non-Defining Clause) - My brother, who works for Samsung, got a new car. (one brother, extra info)

A. Grammar Practice. ***Combine the two sentences by using a relative clause.***

1. The man is an actor. The actor is very handsome.

____

2. My sister is going to visit me. She lives in Brazil.

____

3. This is my friend. He used to go to school with me.

____

4. Steve is a scientist. His daughter is my classmate.

____

5. Did you find the ring? Your father gave it to you.

____

Speaking Skill: Interrupting

Depending on the situation, you can interrupt a conversation using either a formal or informal expression.

Formal	Informal
I'm sorry to interrupt, but...	Hang on. / Hold up.
Sorry for the interruption, but...	Wait a sec. / Just a sec.
Excuse me, but... / Pardon me, but...	Wait a minute...
I'm sorry, but...	Sorry, but...

These expressions should be followed by a complete sentence or question.

I'm sorry to interrupt, but you have a call.

Excuse me, but could you repeat that?

If you'd like to add a comment to the conversation, you can add:

Can I jump in here?

Can I say something?

Practice

A. Role Play. ***Read the following scenarios. Choose one (or create your own!) and write a short role play (6-8 lines) with your group. Use interrupting expressions from above.***

1. You are in a meeting at your company. Your team is discussing ideas for a new product, and you want to add your idea. Interrupt to add your idea.
2. You are at dinner with your friends. A friend is telling a story, but you are confused about the details. Interrupt to ask a question.

Wrap Up

1. Do you think English is a difficult language to learn? Why?

2. Are you studying another language now? If so, which language? If not, which language would you like to learn in the future?

3. Why do people from your country study English?

4. What is the best country to study English in? Why?

5. What are reasons for studying a foreign language?

6. Are there any disadvantages to studying English, or another foreign language?

7. Do you think there is a "Korean English"? If so, do you think it is equally as good as English spoken by native speakers?

8. Do you think there are other "global" languages? Explain.

9. Do you think another language will soon become the new "global language"? If so, which one?

10. **Culture Talk: How has learning English influenced your native language and/or culture?**

UNIT 10

Show Me the Drama

Warm-up *Brainstorming Dramas*

What are the 3 most popular Korean dramas of all time?

1. ________________________________

____

2. ________________________________

____

3. ________________________________

____

Which foreign TV shows are you watching these days?

1. ________________________________

____

2. ________________________________

____

3. ________________________________

____

Vocabulary Focus

A. Definition Matching. ***Write the letter next to the correct word.***

______	1. stage (v.)	C. to speculate about
______	2. theorize (v.)	D. occur again; repeatedly
______	3. exponentially (adv.)	E. tough and graphic
______	4. genre (n.)	F. well known for a bad quality
______	5. recur (v.)	G. to increase (or decrease) more and more rapidly
______	6. gritty (adj.)	H. the quality of being attractive or fascinating
______	7. infamous (adj.)	I. a category of artistic composition
______	8. allure (n.)	J. to produce something for public view

B. Fill in the Blanks. ***Write the correct vocabulary word from above.***

1. The group plans to __________ a protest during the conference.
2. Horror is her favorite movie __________.
3. The cost of housing has increased __________ in the last decade.
4. After hiding from the police for ten years, the __________ criminal was finally caught.
5. Comic books hold a special __________ for collectors.
6. The scientists __________ that pollution could cause hidden health problems.
7. The book depicted the __________ side of the city.
8. You should go back to the doctor if your symptoms start to __________.

Show Me the Drama

Korean dramas are popular around the world, and have found a particularly attentive audience in Mexico. The drama *Star in My Heart*, or Un Deseo en *las Estrellas* in Spanish, was introduced to local audiences in 2002 and ushered in a new era of fandom in Mexico. The Korean wave, or *Hallyu*, took longer to reach Mexico than other countries in East Asia or Southeast Asia, and did not instantly blow up, but over time it has become a powerful subculture in Mexican entertainment.

A major driving force for the popularity of Korean dramas in Mexico is the establishment of fan clubs where Mexicans can communicate with others sharing the same interests. These clubs, such as *HallyuMx* and *Hallyu Mexican Lovers*, stage dance competitions and celebrate the birthdays of their favorite Korean entertainers. This is a fun way for fans to get together to express their love for these shows and entertainers.

Some theorize that Korean dramas have grown exponentially in Mexico as a result of some similarities between them and the massively popular Mexican *telenovelas* which have been around for a long time. Both genres have some common recurring themes, such as working-class melodramas, or rags-to-riches stories, where a poor woman falls in love with a rich man. Additionally, romantic comedies and historical stories set many years in the past are popular in both genres.

Criminal elements appear in both styles too, but they are portrayed very differently. Some telenovelas focus on the grittier side of Mexico's infamous cartels, while Korean criminal dramas tend to be action-packed thrillers. Of course there are many other differences between the two genres as a result of the unique cultures found in South Korea and Mexico.

For many Mexicans, this noticeable difference is precisely what makes Korean dramas so appealing. The plotlines are familiar in some ways, but so different from anything Mexican at the same time. This adds an interesting allure and keeps the fans hungry for more.

Comprehension Check

Complete the Summary

Korean dramas are popular all over the __________, especially in __________. The first major drama was introduced to Mexican audiences in __________ and since then it has become more popular. There are a lot of fan __________ in Mexico where fans can __________ with others sharing the same interest. Some people think there are __________ between Korean dramas and telenovelas. Both genres have __________ themes, but there are also major differences because of the vastly different __________ in South Korea and Mexico. This difference is what makes Korean dramas so __________ for many Mexicans.

True or False

1. Korean dramas were introduced to Mexico in 2002. (T / F)
2. There are fan clubs for Korean dramas in Mexico. (T / F)
3. Rags-to-riches stories are never found in telenovelas. (T / F)
4. Romantic comedies are popular in Korea and Mexico. (T / F)
5. Cultural differences make Korean dramas more interesting for many Mexicans. (T / F)

Let's Discuss

Do you prefer romantic comedies or historical dramas? Why?

Phrasal Verbs:

Get together - Meet / *Blow up* - Become popular quickly

1. Science club is a great way for students to __________ and learn at the same time.
2. It took her a long time to __________, but now she's known all around the world.

Building Communication

Korean Dramas

Pros	Cons

Paragraph Writing: What's your favorite Korean drama? Describe the plot.

Grammar: Adverb (Dependent) Clauses

Dependent (or subordinate) clauses are a subject and verb introduced by a subordinating conjunction. They must be used together with an independent clause, or sentence, in order to make sense. There are several types of subordinate clauses, but we will look at *Adverb Clauses*.

- *Time*: when, whenever, since, until, before, after a while, as by the time, as soon as
  ➜ He said he would call me when he gets home.
- *Cause and effect*: because, since, now that, as long as, so, so that
  ➜ Since you are hungry, you should eat.
- *Contrast*: although, even, whereas, while, though, even though
  ➜ Although Keiko was tired, she still went to the party.
- *Condition*: if, unless, only if, whether or not, even if, in case
  ➜ If you study hard, you can get a good grade.

The independent or the dependent clause can come first, however, if the dependent clause comes first, there must be a comma between the two clauses.

A. ***Complete the sentences below.***

1. I didn't go to the party, *because* ______________________________.
2. *Although* ______________________, we still went to the beach last week.
3. He said that he would buy all his friends a car *if* ____________________.
4. The little girls refused to go to sleep *until* ________________________.

B. **Conditional Shiritori.** ***Take turns making conditional statements. The first person will make a conditional statement, then the second person will use the second clause (independent one) to create a new conditional statement.***

Example:

"If I miss my bus, I will be late for class." ➜ "If I am late for class, I will miss some of the lesson." ➜ "If I miss some of the lesson, I might get a bad grade on my test."

Speaking Skill: Reported Speech

We use Reported Speech to tell someone what another person said. Direct reported speech is someone's exact words, while Indirect isn't their exact words, but conveys the same information.
Direct: My friend said, "The movie was boring."
Indirect: He said that the movie was boring.

When reporting a question, we have to change the question to a sentence, and add the word "if" (Yes/No Question).
Direct: My grandma asked me, "Did you eat lunch?"
Indirect: She asked me if I ate lunch.

A. *Complete the following sentences using direct and indirect.*

Person: Sister Words: "The cafe has a really nice atmosphere."

Direct: ______________________________

Indirect: ______________________________

Person: Uncle Words: "Can I borrow some money?"

Direct: ______________________________

Indirect: ______________________________

B. *Practice reported speech for the following examples. (Use direct and indirect)*

Person	Words
Friend	"The restaurant has really delicious chicken."
Mom	"Did you finish your homework?"
Woman on the street	"Can you tell me how to get to the subway station?"
Boyfriend	"I'm hungry. I want to eat samgyeopsal for dinner."
Professor	"Study chapters 1-6 for the exam."

Wrap Up

1. Do you watch television? If so, what kinds of shows do you watch?

2. Do you only watch TV programs from your country or do you watch shows from other countries?

3. What kinds of television shows are currently popular in your country?

4. Do you think there are advantages to watching television programs?

5. Do you think children should watch dramas? Why or why not?

6. Do you prefer TV programs that have realistic stories or imaginary ones?

7. Do you think all television should be informative or educational? Why or why not?

8. Have you ever watched a telenovela? If not, would you in the future?

9. Do you think TV programs should try to introduce controversial or sensitive topics?

10. **Culture Talk: What type of media is popular in your country that comes from another country or vice versa? Why do you think it's popular?**

UNIT 11

Families are A-Changin'

Warm-up *Sibling Rivalry*

How many siblings do you have? ________________

Choose one sibling and answer these questions:

What is his or her name? ________________

What is one thing that annoys you about your sibling?

____

What is one thing you really love about your sibling?

____

Vocabulary Focus

A. Definition Matching. ***Write the letter next to the correct word.***

_______	1. sibling (n.)	A. money saved for the future
_______	2. labor-force (n.)	B. brother or sister
_______	3. correlation (n.)	C. incapable of being fully understood
_______	4. unfathomable (adj.)	D. the state of not having a job
_______	5. unemployment (n.)	E. a relationship or connection between two things
_______	6. nest egg (n.)	F. a person who earns money to support a family
_______	7. prudent (adj.)	G. showing care and thought for the future
_______	8. breadwinner (n.)	H. all the workers in a population

B. Fill in the Blanks. ***Write the correct vocabulary word from above.***

1. There is a strong ___________ between cold weather and high utility bills.
2. After the baby was born, I became the ___________ of our family.
3. We were not allowed in the restaurant for some ___________ reason.
4. The government is working hard to expand the ___________.
5. A ___________ person always tries to save part of every paycheck.
6. He has a huge family with five ___________.
7. The president bragged about the low ___________ rate.
8. Her retirement ___________ decreased in value by about ten percent.

Families are A-Changin'

Do you have any friends with more than four siblings? Fifty years ago, a family of this size would have been a lot more common than it is today. This is a result of rapidly changing family structures around the world. Over the last few decades, a few major trends have led to lasting cultural changes.

For starters, a massive increase in the number of females entering the labor-force and pursuing higher education has caused many women to delay having children, or to even avoid it altogether. This is a global phenomenon and there is a strong correlation between attaining higher levels of education and delaying childbirth. Accordingly, the average household size has steadily decreased across OECD countries over the last few decades.

Additionally, it is more common for men and women to put off having kids until being fully established in the labor market. Most agree that this is a direct result of the increased competition for jobs and the ever-increasing costs of raising children in most developed economies around the world.

The increased competition for jobs has also led to more children and young adults living at home for longer than before. Many trace this change back to the global financial crisis of 2008 and the economic uncertainty it caused. The financial crisis led to higher unemployment rates in many OECD countries, which in turn caused many recent graduates to move back in with their parents. By living with their parents for a longer time, young adults in today's modern economy are able to build a larger nest egg before stepping out on their own. Some think this is the most prudent choice for young people with an uncertain future, but others think it is important for young people to live on their own and to learn important life skills.

The traditional family, with the father as the breadwinner and the mother staying home to look after the children, is also changing in today's world. Alternatives to the norm are becoming more and more accepted around the world. For example, the phrase *stay-at-home* dad was unfathomable a generation ago, but it is slowly becoming more mainstream. For those who haven't heard of this, it's a family with a female breadwinner, where the father stays home to tend to chores and look after the children.

The next time you talk to a senior citizen, ask them about the changes they've noticed. Most likely they'll have a lot to say.

Comprehension Check

Complete the Summary

Family __________ are changing around the __________. One reason is a large increase in the number of __________ entering the __________. This has caused the average household size to steadily __________ over the last few __________. The cost of raising __________ has been increasing in most __________ economies around the world. The stiff competition for __________ has led to more young people living at __________ than in the past. Many believe this is a result of the financial __________ of 2008. Some people think this is a __________ choice in order to save money. Family structures are changing in other ways too. Nowadays, a father doesn't always have to be the __________ of a family. Stay-at-home dads are becoming more __________ and accepted than in the past.

True or False

1. The average household size has recently increased in all OECD countries. (T / F)
2. More females work now than in the past. (T / F)
3. There is no correlation between higher education and delaying childbirth. (T / F)
4. The financial crisis led to higher unemployment. (T / F)
5. Men are traditionally the breadwinners of a family. (T / F)

Phrasal Verbs:

Tend to - Take care of / *Put off* - Delay, procrastinate

1. I can't __________ my essay any longer. It's due tomorrow.
2. All your flowers are dying. You need to __________ your garden.

Building Communication

Decreasing Household Sizes

Pros	Cons

Paragraph Writing: Would you rather work a normal job or be a stay-at-home mom or dad? Why?

Grammar: Gerunds

Gerunds are verbs that are used as nouns. They look exactly like present participles. Both add "+ing" to the root of a verb. However, gerunds are always used as a noun and present participles are often used as adjectives that modify a noun.

You can find them commonly used in the following ways:

- *As a subject of a sentence*
  → Speaking English is difficult for me.
- *As an object of a sentence*
  → His hobbies are reading, playing games, and writing stories.
- *As a verb complement of the verb "to be"*
  → One of my responsibilities at home is cleaning the bathroom.
- *After prepositions*
  → Jacques is really good at drawing.
- *After phrasal verbs*
  → I gave up playing the game when I started to lose.

A. ***Look at the sentences below. Circle the correct form of the verb to complete the sentence.***

1. Joan keeps on (try/trying) to get a job at the new mall, but they always say they have enough workers right now.
2. Some guy messaged me on a dating app. His profile said that he likes (take/taking) long walks on the beach.
3. Doctors say that one of the things people can do for good heart health is (avoid/avoiding) red meat.
4. (Read/reading) the news is important if you want to (keep/keeping) up to date with what is happening in the world.
5. He plans to lose weight by only (change/changing) his diet.

Speaking Skill: Advice

When we have problems in life, we often need to ask for or give advice. After discussing the problem, we can ask for and give advice.

Asking About the Problem	
What's wrong?	Are you okay?
What's the matter?	Is everything alright?

Asking For Advice	Giving Advice
What do you think?	I think···
What should I do?	You should/have to/must···
What would you do if you were me?	If I were you, I would···

When giving advice or suggestions, should is weaker, while have to and must are a little stronger.

A. ***Read the following problems with your group. Take turns giving advice.***

Problems: I want to hang out with my friends, but I have no money.

I think I'm gaining too much weight.

My major is really difficult. I want to quit school.

I feel really sick. I think I caught a cold.

B. **Role Play.** ***Choose one problem from (A.) (or create your own!) and write a short role play (6-8 lines) with your group. Use advice expressions from above.***

Wrap up

1. What does the typical family structure in your country look like?

2. What does your family structure look like?

3. Would you rather have a large family or a small family? Why?

4. Do you and your parents hold the same views about family structure?

5. Do you think that friends can be family? Why or why not?

6. Do you want to have a family of your own in the future? Why or why not?

7. What are the advantages of starting a family?

8. Are there any downsides to starting a family?

9. Why do you think more people have decided not to have families nowadays?

10. **Culture Talk: Has the family structure in your country changed compared to the past? How so?**

UNIT 12

It's All in the Context

Warm-up *Body Language Challenge*

Write 3 actions using gerunds (Chapter 11). Don't show your group!

Ex. Washing my face.

1. ______________________________

2. ______________________________

3. ______________________________

In your group, take turns acting out each action.
Other group members, try to guess the gerund
using only body language!

Vocabulary Focus

A. Definition Matching. ***Write the letter next to the correct word.***

______	1. communicate (v)		A. move from one place to another
______	2. influence (v.)		B. share or exchange information
______	3. context (n.)		C. stated clearly and in detail
______	4. transfer (v.)		D. the circumstances that form the setting for an event or idea
______	5. non-verbal (adj.)		E. the power to have an effect on someone or something
______	6. explicit (adj.)		F. to conclude from evidence and reasoning
______	7. infer (v.)		G. following in a logical order
______	8. sequential (adj.)		H. not using words or speech

B. Fill in the Blanks. ***Write the correct vocabulary word from above.***

1. Put the files in ___________ order.
2. You are in charge now. You can ___________ the direction of this company.
3. The historical ___________ of this book is very important.
4. You can ___________ the meaning of this word based on the other words in the sentence.
5. Gestures are an example of ___________ communication.
6. Dolphins can ___________ with each other using sound.
7. He gave me ___________ reasons for leaving our company.
8. I need to ___________ money to his bank account before the holiday.

It's All in the Context

Think about all the different people you have communicated with in your life. Was every interaction the same?

Communication is greatly influenced by the context and the people who use it. Some cultures are called "high-context" cultures. They do not say everything explicitly and a lot of information is transferred through non-verbal clues and the context itself. High-context cultures include many countries in Latin America, Asia, the Middle East, and Africa. By contrast, people from "low-context" cultures need to communicate by saying exactly what they want to communicate through specific details. Most Germanic countries, such as English-speaking countries like the United States or Australia, are low-context cultures. If you do not give enough details, you can run into communication problems. However, in high-context cultures, they can infer more information than what you say, so saying too much is not necessary.

The way cultures think about time also has an effect on communication. In "sequential" cultures, they think about time like a line and a resource. They use words like "spend" and "waste" to talk about time. These cultures tend to focus on one thing at a time and make an effort in the present so they can change the future. They also focus on short-term goals. North America and Northern European countries are mostly sequential cultures. By contrast, countries that are "synchronic" think of time like a circle, and believe the past, present, and future are all connected. They try to understand the present and prepare for the future. Synchronic cultures include many Asian, southern European, and South American countries.

Showing emotion while communicating also differs between cultures. Members of "affective" cultures easily show emotions when they communicate. People from these cultures show their emotions openly and quickly, talk loudly, and use their emotions to make decisions. Many Latin and Middle Eastern cultures are considered affective. On the other hand, countries that are "neutral" do not show a lot of the emotions that they feel. They can sometimes be seen as cold, do not make decisions with their emotions, and believe that there is a time and place to show certain emotions. Examples of neutral cultures include many Asian and Anglo-Saxon cultures.

Communicating with people from a culture with a different communication style is important because it can help us understand more about our own cultures and maybe even adapt some new ways of communication. So, try to meet different people and watch out for different communication styles. You may learn something new!

Comprehension Check

Complete the Summary

Communication is how people speak or share __________. It can teach you a lot about other __________. Communication is strongly __________ by context. People communicate differently in __________ parts of the world. High-context cultures transfer a lot of information using __________ clues. In low-context cultures it is important to __________ say what you want the other person to __________. In sequential cultures, people think of time as a __________ and a commodity. Countries that are __________, think of time as a circle. Communicating with people from other cultures can be __________, but it is important to experience it with an __________ mind.

True or False

1. Communication is not influenced by context. (T / F)
2. In high-context cultures people say everything explicitly. (T / F)
3. Most English-speaking cultures are considered high-context. (T / F)
4. North American cultures are generally considered sequential. (T / F)
5. Many Asian countries are synchronic cultures. (T / F)

Let's Discuss

Do you think you fit better in a high-context or low-context culture? Why?

Phrasal Verbs:

Run into - Have, experience / Watch out - Look out for, be careful

1. __________ for bears when you go camping!
2. If you don't practice your script, you may __________ problems when you speak in front of the class.

Building Communication

Low-Context Cultures

Pros	Cons

Paragraph Writing: Have you ever communicated with someone from another culture? Share your experience.

Grammar: Collocations

Collocations are two or more words that are often used together. When these words are used together, they just sound right. If a word is used with the wrong collocation, then it just sounds "wrong" to a native speaker.

Here are the most common types of collocations you should pay attention to:

- adverb + adjective
  → The kids were not fully aware of what was happening.
- adjective + noun
  → The man has blond hair. (not "yellow")
- noun + noun
  → The announcer asked the audience to give a round of applause.
- noun + verb
  → The rain was falling outside the window.
- verb + noun
  → The man was discharged from the hospital.
- verb + expression with preposition
  → She burst into tears when she heard the bad news.
- verb + adverb
  → I vaguely remember what she told me.

A. ***Looking back at the reading, find the underlined words. Then fill in the sentences below with the word's appropriate collocation.***

1. Regardless of the method of communication, it is greatly influenced __________ the context and people who use it.
2. __________ emotion while communicating also differs between differen cultures.
3. If you see people from these cultures communicating, you may notice that they show their emotions openly and quickly, talk __________, and use their emotions to make decisions.

Speaking Skill: How to End a Conversation

There are four parts to ending a conversation: transition, phrase, reply, goodbye. In a conversation, it will look like this:

Transition + Phrase (A)	Alright, well···	+	I've gotta run.
Reply + Goodbye (B)	Okay!	+	Take it easy!

Here are some natural expressions for each of these parts.

Transition	Phrase	Reply	Goodbye
Anyway,	I've gotta go.	Okay.	See ya.
Okay, well,	I'm gonna head out.	Gotcha.	Talk to you later.
Alright,	I'm gonna get going.	Sounds good.	Take care.
Actually,	I have to go study.	Alright.	Cheers!

Practice

A. *Read the following conversations and write an ending using the expressions.*

A: Yeah, the exam was tough. ______________________________.

B: Gotcha. ______________________________.

A: Wow, it's almost 10:00pm. ______________________________.

B: ______________________________.

B. Role Play. *Think about a conversation you had recently and write a short role play (6-8 lines) with your group. Use the expressions above to write an ending for the conversation.*

Wrap Up

1. What communication style does your country have?

   ____

2. Do you show a lot of emotion when speaking? Explain.

   ____

3. If two people speak English but are from different cultures, could they still have problems communicating? Give an example.

   ____

4. Has technology changed how people from your country communicate?

   ____

5. Do you think people of the same culture have different communication styles? Give an example.

   ____

6. Have you ever had a misunderstanding with someone from another culture because you have different communication styles?

   ____

7. Do you communicate the same way as your parents? What about your grandparents?

   ____

8. Do you communicate now the same way you did when you were a kid?

   ____

9. Do you think people from your country will communicate differently in the future? Why or why not?

   ____

10. **Culture Talk: What are some difficulties you have had when talking to people from other countries?**

    ____

References

Unit 1: Different Strokes for Different Folks

- De Voogt, Alex. "Mancala." *Penn Museum*, Penn Museum, 15 Mar. 2001, https://www.penn.museum/sites/expedition/mancala/.
- Kurumatani, Norio, et al. "Relationship of Having Hobbies and a Purpose in Life With Mortality, Activities of Daily Living, and Instrumental Activities of Daily Living Among Community-Dwelling Elderly Adults." *Journal of Epidemiology*, Japan Epidemiological Association, 5 July 2016, https://www.jstage.jst.go.jp/article/jea/26/7/26_JE20150153/_article/-char/ja/.
- Rossen, Jake. "By Pawn or by Brawn: Inside the Chessboxing Movement." *Mental Floss*, 9 Apr. 2018, https://www.mentalfloss.com/article/501360/chessboxing-movement.
- "Sepak Takraw - Overview." *Tutorialspoint*, https://www.tutorialspoint.com/sepak_takraw/sepak_takraw_overview.htm.

Unit 2: It's a Celebration

- "Bloomsday." T*he James Joyce Centre*, https://jamesjoyce.ie/bloomsday/.
- "Burns Night: Traditions and Robert Burns Information." *Scotland.org*, https://www.scotland.org/events/burns-night.
- Chavez-Bush, Leigh. "The Festival That Honors Monkeys With an Epic Banquet." Atlas Obscura, *Atlas Obscura*, 5 Dec. 2018, https://www.atlasobscura.com/foods/monkey-buffet-festival.
- History.com Editors. "Day of the Dead (Día De Los Muertos)." *History.com*, A&E Television Networks, 30 Oct. 2018, https://www.history.com/topics/halloween/day-of-the-dead.
- "Holiday | Origin and meaning of holiday by Online Etymology Dictionary." *Online Etymology Dictionary | Origin, History and Meaning of English Words*, Douglas Harper, https://www.etymonline.com/word/holiday.
- "Ice Cream For Breakfast Day." *Days Of The Year*, https://www.daysoftheyear.com/days/ice-cream-for-breakfast-day/.
- Wikipedia contributors. "Christianity and paganism." *Wikipedia, The Free Encyclopedia.*

Wikipedia, The Free Encyclopedia, https://www.wikipedia.org/

Unit 3: What's Cookin'?

- Gadsby, Patricia. "The Inuit Paradox." *Discover Magazine*, Discover Magazine, 25 Nov. 2019, https://www.discovermagazine.com/health/the-inuit-paradox.
- Greger, Michael. "Plant-Based Diets for Improved Mood and Productivity." *YouTube*, NutritionFacts.org, 18 Sept. 2015, https://www.youtube.com/watch?v=U9rx9wQrVdk.
- Singh, Maanvi. "Is Samoa's Obesity Epidemic A Harbinger For Other Developing Nations?" *NPR*, NPR, 7 Apr. 2016, https://www.npr.org/sections/thesalt/2016/04/07/473371279/is-samoa-s-obesity-epidemic-a-harbinger-for-other-developing-nations.
- Streit, Lizzie. "Carnivore Diet Review: Benefits, Downsides, and Sample Menu." *Healthline*, Healthline Media, 26 Aug. 2019, https://www.healthline.com/nutrition/carnivore-diet.
- "The Vegan Diet." *NHS Choices*, NHS,https://www.nhs.uk/live-well/eat-well/the-vegan-diet/.

Unit 4: Pride and Prejudices

- Desmond-Harris, Jenée. "What Exactly Is a Microaggression?" *Vox*, Vox, 16 Feb. 2015, https://www.vox.com/2015/2/16/8031073/what-are-microaggressions.
- Grierson, Jamie. "Landlord Investigated over 'Disgusting Remark' about 'Coloured' People." *The Guardian*, Guardian News and Media, 28 Mar. 2017, https://www.theguardian.com/society/2017/mar/28/landlord-fergus-wilson-said-coloured-people-leave-curry-smell.
- Williams, Jessica. "'Secretaries Are Women, That's How It's Always Been'." *The Guardian*, Guardian News and Media, 17 Oct. 2016, https://www.theguardian.com/small-business-network/2016/oct/17/secretaries-acceptable-sexism-women-workplace.

Unit 5: Birds of a Feather Flock Together

- Light, Alan, and Greg Tate. "Hip-Hop." *Encyclopædia Britannica*, Encyclopædia

Britannica, Inc., 12 Dec. 2019, https://www.britannica.com/art/hip-hop.

- Lyons, Juliette. "La Sape : an Elegance That Brought Peace in the Midst of Congolese Chaos." *Le Journal International - Archives*, Le Journal International, 12 May 2014, https://www.lejournalinternational.fr/La-Sape-an-elegance-that-brought-peace-in-the-midst-of-Congolese-chaos_a1871.html.
- McCrystal, Hayley. "The History of Motorcycle Culture ." *MotorbikeTimes*, MotorbikeTimes, 12 Aug. 2014, http://www.motorbiketimes.com/feature/the-history-of-motorcycle-culture-$21384141.htm
- Moffitt, Kimberly. "What Is Subculture? - Theories, Definition & Examples." *Study.com*, Study.com, https://study.com/academy/lesson/what-is-subculture-theories-definition-examples.html
- Patterson, Thom. "Inside the Misunderstood Culture of Furries." *CNN*, Cable News Network, 14 Nov. 2018, https://edition.cnn.com/2018/11/14/us/furries-culture/index.html.
- The Editors of Encyclopaedia Britannica. "Hippie." *Encyclopædia Britannica*, Encyclopædia Britannica, Inc., 23 Aug. 2002, https://www.britannica.com/topic/hippie.
- Wikipedia contributors. "History of the punk subculture." *Wikipedia, The Free Encyclopedia*. Wikipedia, The Free Encyclopedia, https://www.wikipedia.org/
- "Yami-Kawaii Harajuku Subculture in Japan." *TokyoTreat*, TokyoTreat, 15 Aug. 2018, https://tokyotreat.com/news/yami-kawaii-japan.

Unit 6: A Whole New (Digital) World

- Gray, Alex. "The Explosive Growth of ESports." *World Economic Forum*, 3 July 2018, https://www.weforum.org/agenda/2018/07/the-explosive-growth-of-esports/.
- Lopez, German. "ASMR, Explained: Why Millions of People Are Watching YouTube Videos of Someone Whispering." *Vox*, Vox, 25 May 2018, https://www.vox.com/2015/7/15/8965393/asmr-video-youtube-autonomous-sensory-meridian-response.

Unit 7: Getting on Up There in Years

- Boyer, Paul. "Young and Old Alike: Children and the Elderly Are a Priority in Native American Cultures." *Tribal College Journal of American Indian Higher Education*, American Indian Higher Education Consortium, 15 Feb. 1992, https://tribalcollegejournal.org/young-alike-children-elderly-priority-native-american-cultures/.

- Bryant, Sue. "Death and Dying: How Different Cultures View the End." *Country Navigator*, Country Navigator, 2 Sept. 2019, https://countrynavigator.com/blog/cultural-intelligence/death/.
- DiGiulio, Sarah. "What Is 'Swedish Death Cleaning' and Should You Be Doing It?" *NBCNews.com*, NBCUniversal News Group, 10 Jan. 2018, https://www.nbcnews.com/better/health/what-swedish-death-cleaning-should-you-be-doing-it-ncna816511.
- Gregoire, Carolyn. "How Changing The Way You Think About Death Can Transform The Way You Live." *HuffPost*, HuffPost, 29 Aug. 2013, https://www.huffpost.com/entry/how-changing-the-way-you-_n_3790274.
- History.com Editors. "Day of the Dead (Día De Los Muertos)." *History.com*, A&E Television Networks, 30 Oct. 2018, https://www.history.com/topics/halloween/day-of-the-dead.
- Mancini, Mark. "Ghana's Fantasy Coffins Are to Die For." *HowStuffWorks*, HowStuffWorks, 29 Oct. 2019, https://people.howstuffworks.com/culture-traditions/funerals/ghana-fantasy-coffins.htm.
- Mbugua, Johnson Nganga. "Nigeria-The Urhobo People." *Funeral Rites Reformation for Any African Ethnic Community Based on the Proposed New Funeral Practices for the Agikyuyu*, Wipf and Stock Publishers, 2016, p. 63. Google Books, https://books.google.co.kr/books?id=DE-DDAAAQBAJ&pg=PA63&lpg=PA63&dq=urhobo of nigeria good death.
- Meyers, Karen. "Ethnic Rituals and Death." *The Truth About Death and Dying*, edited by Robert N. Golden, 2nd ed., DWJ Books LLC, 2009, p. 101. Google Books, https://books.google.co.kr/books?id=V-wan_XhkzcC&pg=PA101&lpg=PA101&dq=ronald k barrett "natural rhythm of life"
- "Traditional Korean Holiday of Bountiful Harvest, Chuseok." *Traditional Korean Holiday of Bountiful Harvest, Chuseok | Official Korea Tourism Organization*, Korea Tourism Organization, 2 Sept. 2019, https://english.visitkorea.or.kr/enu/ATR/SI_EN_3_6.jsp?cid=811650.

Unit 8: Making the Grade

- Beaubien, Jason. "'Floating Schools' Make Sure Kids Get To Class When The Water Rises." *NPR*, NPR, 12 Sept. 2018, https://www.npr.org/sections/goatsandsoda/2018/09/12/646378073/floating-schools-mak

e-sure-kids-get-to-class-when-the-water-rises.

- "Malala Yousafzai Biographical." *NobelPrize.org*, Nobel Media, 2014, https://www.nobelprize.org/prizes/peace/2014/yousafzai/biographical/.
- Ranjani Balaji Iyer. "Blending East and West for holistic education." Educational Research and Reviews 10.3 (2015): 244-248.
- "What Are the Key Barriers to Education in Developing Countries?" *The Digital Age*, University of New South Wales, 16 Apr. 2018, https://blogs.unsw.edu.au/thedigitalage/blog/2018/04/what-are-the-key-barriers-to-education-in-developing-countries/.

Unit 9: The Language Heard 'Round the World

- Eberhard, David M., Gary F. Simons, and Charles D. Fennig (eds.). 2019. *Ethnologue: Languages of the World*. Twenty-second edition. Dallas, Texas: SIL International. Online version: http://www.ethnologue.com.

Unit 10: Show Me the Drama

- Lopez Rocha, Nayelli. *Hallyu in Mexico and the Role of Korean Pop Idols' Fan Clubs*. The Journal of Foreign Studies, June 2013, http://congress.aks.ac.kr/korean/files/2_1357264037.pdf.

Unit 11: Families are A-Changin'

- OECD (2011), "Families are changing", in *Doing Better for Families*, OECD Publishing, Paris,https://doi.org/10.1787/9789264098732-3-en.

Unit 12: It's All in the Context

- "Getting Angry at Work: Affective and Neutral Cultures." *CAL Learning*, CAL Learning, 10 June 2010, https://www.callearning.com/blog/2010/06/getting-angry-at-work-affective-and-neutral-cultures/.
- "Intercultural Communication: High and Low Context Cultures." *Southeastern University Online*, Southeastern University Online, 18 Aug. 2016,

https://online.seu.edu/articles/high-and-low-context-cultures/.

- "Sequential or Synchronic?" *InterCultural English*, https://www.ic-english.com/sequentialsynchronic.html.

Images:

- https://pixabay.com/

The Big Picture

English for a Globally Connected World